Ephesians

7 Lessons for Group or Individual Study

Real World Bible Study

Joy Suzanne Hunt

To my grandfathers, who taught me to love God's Word and inspired me with your mission to make it available to the nations.

How to Use This Study

How to Use This Study

Real World Bible Study guides make it easy to build a daily Bible study habit and learn to understand God's Word for yourself. You can use this study on your own or with a group (and this study includes recommendations for both). I recommend a pattern of daily independent study, combined with a weekly time for fellowship and discussion.

The Intro Session (Week 1) will provide the first meeting to launch your group; members do not need to prepare anything before the first session. The leader should read through the

Intro Session material ahead of time to be ready to facilitate the discussion. This session will help you familiarize yourself with the book of Ephesians and the structure of this study. It also provides an excellent opportunity for small group leaders to walk members through key aspects of your small group and lay out expectations, answer questions, and foster a positive group atmosphere. .

Each week contains five daily studies (complete these on your own or with your family), followed by a group session. If you are studying alone, you can use the group session as a time of personal reflection.

Often readers struggle knowing where to begin with a Bible study. This study is designed to allow readers to jump in at any level--to take on as little or as much as they desire. By embracing the idea that it doesn't need to be all or nothing, the format creates space for readers to grow a daily study habit each day and week.

* * *

How Much Do I Need to Do Each Week?

This decision is between you and God - and it may look different from week to week and season to season as you navigate the challenges of daily life. When we touch God's Word every day, we will reap the benefits.Think of these as building blocks–use as many as you need.

- If you can do just one thing, show up to your group study each week, read with the group, and take part in the discussion.
- If you add one more thing to that, complete the assigned reading each day. This should only take a few minutes.
- If you add one more thing to that, complete the **Study** section each day. This should take about 15 minutes.
- Want more time in the Word? Complete the optional **Go Deeper** section, which can take as long as you choose!
- Each week also includes a memory verse; you can spend as little or as much time on these as you wish. You can find ideas for Scripture memorization at

RealWorldBibleStudy.com/memory-verse-activities.

What Do I Need to Study the Bible?

All you need is a Bible in a good translation that you can understand. Some of my favorites include the NLT, NIV and CEB. Check out *How to Read the Bible for All Its Worth* by Stuart and Fee for a great chapter on the differences between translations.

E-Bibles are great for audio listeners and exploring different translations, but for personal Bible study, it's better to have a physical paper Bible. Without a screen, you will find it easier to focus and switch between verses and resources.

I recommend a Study Bible if you want to take your Bible Study to the next level. A good study Bible will include background information on each book to help you understand the context. Study Bibles often contain footnotes to explain difficult verses, as well as other resources to help you understand the Bible. Here are a few of my favorite study Bibles:

- Fire Bible

- NLT Study Bible
- NIV Study Bible
- Life Application Study Bible

Another great resource is a journaling Bible. These are Bibles with lots of extra room for taking notes. You can find some of my favorites at https://www.realworldbiblestudy.com/bible-journaling-tools/

You'll also want to keep your favorite pens and highlighters handy (look for the "no-bleed" ones), and a notebook if you are using the e-book version of this study (or just need more room to write!).

Finally, it helps to have a set time and place to complete your daily study. It doesn't need to be fancy. If your "place" isn't somewhere you can leave your "tools" out every day, try a dedicated box or bag. (Personally, I incorporate both options: I have a space where I do my Bible study every day, and I also keep a tote bag for my Bible study items for when I need to take my study somewhere else.)

* * *

Framework: How to Interpret a Bible Passage

Can you just open the Bible and understand what it means, or do you need someone to interpret it for you? What do you think?

Try to interpret this verse:

> οτι ουκ εστιν ημιν η παλη προς αιμα και σαρκα αλλα προς τας αρχας προς τας εξουσιας προς τους κοσμοκρατορας του σκοτους τουτου προς τα πνευματικα της πονηριας εν τοις επουρανιοις.[1]

(Unless you know ancient Greek, you'll need a little help!).

Both sides are true, right? On the one hand, Scripture is for everyone. The Holy Spirit speaks to us while we read to help us understand, and there are some things in Scripture that are easy to interpret. "Children, obey your parents because you belong to the Lord, for this is the right thing to do." (Ephesians 6:1) This is easy to interpret. (Harder to do!)

On the other hand, most of us don't speak ancient Greek! And we don't usually know very much off the top of our heads about what was going on 2000 years ago (what we call "context"). And sometimes, we think that thought came from God when it really didn't. **We interpret Scripture with the help of the Holy Spirit and as part of a community**, so that we can catch each other's bloopers. That community includes your pastors, small group, authors of the books you read, and Bible scholars. And it also includes the people from our community history who have studied God's Word over thousands of years. Good news: anyone can interpret the Bible with some of the right tools, and we have access to more tools than any generation before us.

* * *

The Most Important Tool: A Good Translation (or a few)

Assuming that ancient Greek or Hebrew isn't your first language (fun fact, it isn't anyone's anymore!), one of the most important tools for good interpretation is a **good translation!** Since no language conveys the richness of ancient Hebrew or Greek, it's best to have a few good translations on hand. There's not an exact way to translate, and so translators have to interpret the text and prayerfully decide the best way to say that in English. Isn't it cool that God used humans both to write his Word and make it accessible to each of us in our own languages?

Using different translations will help us gain a clearer understanding of the text. Some of my favorites include the New International Version (NIV), Common English Bible (CEB), and New Living Translation (NLT). (This book uses the NLT unless otherwise noted).

Throughout this study, we will follow a three-step framework to interpret a Bible passage.

- Step 1: What did it mean back then when it was written? (What was the original, intended meaning?)
- Step 2: What does it mean in the light of the rest of Scripture (especially Jesus)?
- Step 3: What does it mean in my life and community now?

Step 1: What did it mean back then when it was written?

This step is often called "exegesis." This step is very important, because a Bible text **"can't mean what it never meant."**[2] Or "the true meaning of the biblical text for us is what God originally intended it to mean when it was first spoken."[3] So how do we figure out what it originally meant? We need to look first at the **context**.

Questions to understand the context:

Historical Context:

- What was going on when the events in Scripture happened? (For example, what was going on in the Roman empire when Jesus was alive?)
- Was there a time gap between when the events happened and when someone wrote about it? If so, how long was that time gap? What was going on when someone wrote about it later? Why did the Holy Spirit inspire someone to write this book? Why did the Holy Spirit inspire the author to write it to this audience at this time? (For example, what was going on in the Roman Empire when the Holy Spirit inspired Luke to write his Gospel a few decades after Jesus' resurrection?)

Literary Context:

- What type of writing is this? (Genre: is it a letter, a historical record, a parable, poetry, or song, etc?) Are there any special things to consider when we interpret this type of writing?
- Who wrote it? (We don't always know!)
- What comes before or after this writing in the text? How does it fit into the rest of this book?
- How does this passage or book relate to other parts of the Bible?

Where can you find the answers to questions like these? Some great resources include a study Bible and a study guide like this one. You can find a list of recommended resources here: https://www.realworldbiblestudy.com/biblestudylibrary.

We may not be able to answer all of these questions, but working to answer them to the best of our ability will help us understand the original meaning correctly.

Step 2: What does it mean in light of the rest of Scripture (especially Jesus)?

For this question, we'll look at how the rest of Scripture addresses similar themes and topics. There are some things that Scripture teaches the same way (or in very similar ways) to different communities in different times. But the Bible teaches other things (like laws about food) in different ways to different communities. Studying a text with the rest of Scripture in mind can help us understand if this is a teaching for all time or only for certain situations. It can also help us understand how the Old Testament and New Testament relate to each other.

Step 3: What does it mean in my life and community now?

The here and now is important—it's what we have to deal with every day. So why don't we start there? The original meaning is the "control;" it's the way we make sure we aren't going off the deep end. Otherwise, we can make a text mean anything we want it to. But it won't be true. When we understand the passage the way the first hearers would understand it, and we've examined it alongside the rest of Scripture, we can connect it to our own lives. We'll ask questions like: how am I like the people in the story? How am I different? What situation might this be like in my world? What is God calling me to do in response?

This study walks you through these types of questions to help you understand God's Word from the inside out, and watch him change *you* from the inside out!

> Now all glory to God, who is able, through his mighty power at work within us, to accomplish infinitely more than we might ask or think.
>
> — Ephesians 3:20

---

1. Westcott & Hort, 2009
2. Fee & Stuart, 2014
3. Fee & Stuart, 2014

How to Lead a Small Group Bible Study

Choose a Time and Place

Your small group may choose to meet in a home, in your workplace, at your church, or in a public place, such as a coffee shop. You'll want to consider whether you need a space for kids and whether you plan to spend time in worship or other activities which might be easier in a home.

Decide whether kids will take part in your group or if you want to provide child care (check with your church staff on the requirements if you are considering childcare provisions). If kids will attend your small group, involve them in some of your activities even if you have a babysitter. For example, even if kids are not taking part in your study, they might join you for worship or for prayer.

Before Your Small Group

Getting ready for your Bible study should not require much extra prep time. If you have done the personal study throughout the week on your own or with your family, you will be 90% of the way there!

- Pray for your small group meeting and for your members by name.
- Complete your personal study in this study guide.
- Read through the Group Session for the week and decide which questions you will use or if any need to be adapted to your group's needs.
- Reach out to your Small Group members the day before or the day of your meeting to make sure everyone knows when and where to meet.

* * *

Small Group Meeting Structure:

The core element of your small group meeting is discussion about the assigned Bible passage, but here are some other elements you may want to include:

- Fellowship/catch-up time
- Food (light snacks and drinks or even a shared meal)
- An icebreaker question
- Worship time (you can have someone lead or create a YouTube playlist in advance).
- Prayer time

Leading the Meeting

- Start with an icebreaker
- Use the Group Session in your study guide to lead the discussion.
- Encourage your group members to invite friends and family members. Remind them each week!

Ask questions, and allow space for silence. Leave room for the group to answer. Your job is to facilitate the discussion, not to know every answer.

- It's okay to say "I don't know, but I can find out."
- Keep an eye out for group members that would make great future leaders. Give them opportunities to lead alongside you. Give them ways to contribute (bring snacks, lead worship, pray, co-lead the discussion with you).
- Keep the group on topic; you may need to redirect the conversation. Keep an ear out for gossip. Shut down gossip gently but firmly.
- Make sure everyone in the group has a chance to speak. A great way to do this can be to ask a question where each person in the room answers.
- Show respect for the opinions of others.

After the Meeting

Follow up with absentees to check in on them. Tell them you missed them!

Introduction to Ephesians

When opening a book, an email, or even this study guide, you can easily identify the original target audience, purpose of writing, and the intended meaning (within reason). Your email shows the sender, the recipients, a timestamp, and a subject line. This study guide shows a copyright date and describes its purpose. These elements help us understand what we're reading. You'll interpret an email from your boss differently from a suspense novel (I hope!).

Ancient literature is the same in that all these pieces are helpful to us while we interpret. And ancient literature is also different: often the authors didn't include these orienting details in their writings. These simply weren't part of the writing conventions of the time, making our first step of interpretation more challenging. (For more on the steps of interpretation, see How to Interpret a Bible Passage.)

In ancient times, there were no copyright dates or informational blurbs on the back cover. They didn't even *have* back covers! The author of Ephesians didn't put a timestamp on this letter. He didn't state his purpose. He told us his name, but not very much about his audience. (Ephesians is a *letter* - the audience already knew who the audience was!)

This introduction provides background information for our study of Ephesians, so we can hear it the way the first audience understood it, and apply it to our lives.

Author

The author identifies himself as the Apostle Paul.[1] You can read the book of Acts, especially starting with chapter 9, to discover Paul's[2] background and how he came to follow Jesus and become the most famous missionary in history, the missionary to the Gentiles. Most of us would not be reading this book or studying God's word or have a relationship with God if not for Paul's work. If you are not familiar with Paul, here's a quick summary:

- Paul was born in Tarsus, a Roman citizen of Jewish descent.
- He underwent formal Jewish religious training in Jerusalem.
- At first, Paul believed the Gospel was heresy. He persecuted the early Christians and hunted down followers of Jesus to have them arrested, beaten, and killed.
- Paul had a life-changing encounter with Jesus in a vision on the road to Damascus one day, which caused him to repent and be baptized. He began preaching about Jesus, but at first, the disciples did not trust his conversion. He then went away to study for an extended time before the Antioch church commissioned him and Barnabas to take the Gospel to the Gentiles.

- Paul planted churches throughout Asia Minor (modern day Turkey) and Greece on multiple missionary journeys. He wrote many of the New Testament letters we love. The book of Acts does not tell us the end of his story; it leaves us with Paul teaching while imprisoned in Rome and awaiting trial.

Genre:

The book of Ephesians is an epistle (a special type of letter): "an artistic literary form...that was intended for the public."[3] Epistles and more personal letters are what we call "occasional documents," meaning that they are written to address a *particular occasion* (see below), usually "some kind of behavior that needed correcting, or a doctrinal error that needed setting right, or a misunderstanding that needed further light."[4]

This letter is a circular letter (meant to be circulated to many churches), and it reads much like a sermon in its style (like a sermon packaged inside a letter).[5] It was likely intended to be read aloud to the churches "in the context of worship and prayer."[6]

Recipients:

You'll notice that it's called "Letter to the Ephesians," and the first verse is addressed to the church at Ephesus. For those of us familiar with Paul's letters, this letter may seem a little strange because it lacks the personal greetings we expect. Paul planted the church at Ephesus and spent three years there. If this letter was only for that specific community, Paul would have included those personal greetings.

The oldest manuscripts of the letter that have been found are missing the words "in Ephesus" in the introduction, and some scholars believe the writer may have left an intentional blank space there. As a circular letter, it was intended to be taken to all the churches in the area surrounding Ephesus, including the Ephesian church. The name of each particular community would replace the words "in Ephesus."[7]

These churches, consisting mostly of Gentile believers (believers not from a Jewish background), are like Paul's "grandchild churches." Paul ("father") planted the church at Ephesus (child) and raised up leaders there who took the gospel to the surrounding area and planted churches (grandchild churches) in many of the 230 independent communities within the Roman province of Asia.[8]

Time, Setting, Occasion:

Paul tells us that he is writing from prison. He doesn't tell us *which* prison or which time he was in prison (Paul spent time in prison on multiple occasions!), but it seems most likely that this letter was written during Paul's long imprisonment in Rome, around AD 62.

The letter itself does not give us any direct clues to the occasion or reason that Paul is writing the letter, but it does help to read it alongside its sister letter, the Letter to the Colossians. As we will discuss, these two letters have a very close relationship, and reading one can help us to understand the other. For now it is enough to say that unlike many of Paul's other letters, the book of Ephesians was not written to address a specific problem in a specific church. It may have been written to address issues that had come up in multiple churches for a broader audience, especially division caused by false teachers.

Historical Context:

As mentioned before, Paul planted the church in Ephesus, stayed there for a few years, and raised up leadership. Eventually, he continued on with his missionary work elsewhere. One convert from the church at Ephesus was a man named Epaphras, who went on to plant churches in the surrounding area, including Colossae. Epaphras visited Paul in prison and brought to Paul some concerns that the church in Colossae was struggling with, especially division caused by false teaching. Paul wrote the letter to the Colossians to firmly address the specific issues that the Colossian church was facing.[9]

Why are we talking so much about the Colossian church? Isn't this study about Ephesians? Well, Ephesians quotes Colossians extensively.[10] It appears that after writing Colossians (to a *specific church* to address *specific issues*), Paul expanded it to write a much more general letter to all the churches in the surrounding area to prepare them to address those the same issues.[11] We know this letter as Ephesians. So the "occasion" for Ephesians closely relates to that of Colossians.

In Colossae, the false teachers were beginning to cause division. There were errors in theology, especially around rules and regulations; some were "putting pressure on Gentile believers to conform to Jewish identity markers (circumcision, food laws, religious calendar)."[12] These pressures were mixed with an unhealthy emphasis on spiritual rulers, powers, and secret knowledge, taking away from the role of Christ in daily life and in salvation. These teachings also "seem[ed] to be in conflict with the physical side of Christ's earthly life and redemption."[13] The Colossian church (like other New Testament churches) was engaging with a cultural movement that we call proto-Gnosticism.

Gnosticism is a movement that became more developed in the first and second centuries. What we see in New Testament times is not that fully developed version. And unfortunately, we don't have clear writings about Gnostic ideas from this early time, but we can definitely see what we would call proto-Gnostic ideas in the culture that Paul and the other New Testament writers encountered and responded to as they wrote their instructions for the early Church.

Features of Proto-Gnosticism:

Gnosticism (both in its early and fully developed forms) was a cultural movement that penetrated many religions and many religious communities, not just one. The early Christians were no exception.

A key feature of Gnosticism was the idea of dualism, or the separation between spirit and matter. Spirit was regarded as "good" and matter as "bad" or "evil." As a material creation, the body "was regarded as inherently evil."[14] Since they believed physical matter to be evil, most Gnostics "held that Christ did not truly suffer as he was not truly incarnate"[15] (fully human). This, of course, flies in the face of the Genesis 1 description of creation as "good" and makes a mockery of Christ's *physical* sacrifice on the cross.

Gnostics believed that seven angelic levels existed between a holy high God and a lesser evil "god" who created matter. In their view, the path to salvation involved passing through these levels and was only available to some through a special secret knowledge or mystery ("gnosis").[16] For people influenced by these ideas, the *source* of salvation became human knowledge rather than divine grace.

As a result, ethics usually went in either one of two directions, both of which are incorrect according to the New Testament writers. Some people influenced by proto-Gnosticism were legalistic because matter is "bad," and one must control it by living a very ascetic or strict life.[17] Or on the other end of the spectrum, if matter is "bad" and spirit is "good" and they are completely separate, then what happens with your body doesn't matter at all. They believed that ethics have nothing to do with your spiritual life. Some Gnostics "indulged deliberately" in promiscuous behavior and "urged [their] followers to take part in all sins."[18]

Paul addressed both perspectives in many of his writings, and especially in the book of Ephesians. He emphasizes that salvation is not something that we cause. It is not something that comes from our own knowledge. It is a gift from God that none of us can boast about (Ephesians 2:8-

10). As you read through the book of Ephesians, think about this original culture and what they would have heard as these words were read to them.

Purpose:

As noted above, Paul doesn't actually tell us the purpose of his letter. But from our study of the context and the book, we can infer that Paul has two reasons for writing Ephesians:

1. He expands on the concerns he has for the Colossians to address a general audience, making sure that these new generations of churches, these "grandchild churches," have a correct understanding of <u>what to believe</u> and <u>how to live</u>. Remember, these early churches don't have the whole Bible like we do. And they no longer have Paul there teaching.
2. He beautifully tells the ultimate story of God's plan for redemption and reconciliation, and how that works out in a practical way in our lives.

Themes to Watch For:

1. Salvation for Gentiles was God's plan from the beginning.
2. We are to live a different life from those around us, set apart, that honors God and each other.
3. Spirit filled relationships and how they should operate.
4. Unity is the common thread that seems to tie the entire book together.
5. Spiritual warfare: Who is the real enemy and how do we fight?

---

1. Some scholars believe this letter may have been written at a later date by a follower of Paul. For more details on the argument, see Klein, et al., 2017
2. In the beginning of Paul's story in Acts, he is called his Hebrew name Saul. When he begins to serve as a missionary among Gentiles, the author switches to referring to him by his Greek name, Paul.
3. Fee, & Stuart, 2014
4. Fee, & Stuart, 2014
5. Klein, et al., 2017
6. Patzia, 2011
7. Patzia, 2011
8. Longman, et al., 2006
9. Klein, et al., 2017

10. For chart comparing the two letters, see Klein, et al., 2017
11. Klein, et al., 2017
12. Fee, 2009
13. Fee, 2009
14. Hawthorne, et al., 1993
15. Hawthorne, et al., 1993
16. Tyndale, 2008 "Introduction to the New Testament"
17. Hawthorne, et al., 1993
18. Hawthorne, et al., 1993

Week 1: Intro Session

Group Session

Leaders: Give members an overview of how you will run the group sessions and what they will do at home. You may want to talk about worship or other activities your group will do together, as well as logistical items like snacks, parking, or child care.

Opening Prayer:

Ask God to guide your conversation as you study his Word together.

What to Expect from this Study:

Today will be an overview and introduction to the book of Ephesians. Going forward, you'll be completing 5 days of study on your own each week, followed by our group discussion. For more information about the structure of this study, see How to Use This Study and How to Study the Bible at the beginning of this book. For your study at home each week, feel free to choose how much time to spend each day.

- If you can only do one thing, do the group session with us each week.
- If you can do a little more, complete the reading each day.
- If you can do even a little more, complete the reading and study each day.
- If you can do a little more than that, complete the reading, study, "Go Deeper," and other activities each day.

That being said, our group discussions will be more interesting if we've each had some time to let God's Word simmer and soak throughout the week, so try to spend a little time every day.

Each weekly session will include a memory verse for us to practice together, reading, discussion around the week's reading, and time for prayer.

Memory Verse Activity:

"I have not stopped thanking God for you. I pray for you constantly, asking God, the glorious Father of our Lord Jesus Christ, to give you spiritual wisdom and insight so that you might grow in your knowledge of God."

— Ephesians 1:16-17 NLT

Practice this verse as a group. If you need ideas for ways to practice, see the list of Memory Verse Activities at RealWorldBibleStudy.com/memory-verse-activities.

Discussion:

1. What do you hope to get out of this Bible study?
2. What do you know about the book of Ephesians, if anything? If you have read

it before, what do you remember about this book?

Reading:

Orienting Details:

- Author: Paul, when he was in prison (most likely in prison in Rome)
- Recipients: Many churches in the area surrounding Ephesus.

(We'll learn more about the background and context of Ephesians this week.)

Read Ephesians chapters 1-6 together as a group. This will help get a big-picture overview of the book. As you read, have a pen/highlighter in hand to capture questions or points that stand out to you.

Discussion:

Use the questions below to direct your group discussion, and/or add your own. Make sure each group member has an opportunity to share.

If you're studying independently, use the questions below for journaling/reflection.

1. What was one thing that stood out to you or surprised you as you read Ephesians? Or what was your favorite part?
2. Why do you think Paul wrote Ephesians? What do you think are some major themes?
3. What questions do you have that you would like to answer over the next six weeks?
4. What do you want to do this week in response to God's Word?

Prayer:

Depending on the size of your group, you may choose to pray together as a group or break off into pairs or smaller groups to share prayer requests. If you're studying independently, use this time to talk to God about what he has spoken to you through this chapter.

Week 2: Ephesians 1

Day 1: Getting Oriented

Begin with Prayer:

Invite God to speak to you as you read his Word. Ask God to help you understand, remember, and follow his Word.

Reading:

Read the Introduction to Ephesians at the beginning of this book. Today's study will provide some background to the book of Ephesians to help you understand this letter in its original context.

Study:

1. What features from the historical context of Ephesians were most surprising to you? Which ones have parallels with your own community or context?

----

2. What was Paul's purpose in writing Ephesians? Which purpose from the text stands out to you or makes you most curious and why?

----

3. What is God saying to you through your study today?

Go Deeper (optional):

Ephesians is a letter, and no part of it is meant to be interpreted on its own. We need to understand how the whole letter fits together and interpret it as a whole, not just individual verses. Create an outline of the book of Ephesians. This will give you a big picture of the book's content. You can skim through the chapters and start from scratch, or use an outline from your favorite study Bible. Either way, writing the outline will help you consider the overall structure of Paul's letter.

Write your outline here:

Memory Verse:

Practice/review Ephesians 1:5. For ideas to help learn the verse, see RealWorldBible-Study.com/memory-verse-activities.

> "God decided in advance to adopt us into his own family by bringing us to himself through Jesus Christ. This is what he wanted to do, and it gave him great pleasure."
>
> — Ephesians 1:5

Prayer

Talk to God about what you think he is saying to you today. Ask for his help to live out his Word. You may want to write your prayer here or in a journal.

* * *

Day 2: Ephesians 1:1-14

Begin with Prayer:

Invite God to speak to you as you read his Word. Ask God to help you understand, remember, and follow his Word.

Reading:

Read Ephesians 1:1-14.

Study:

Step 1: What did it mean "back then" when it was written?

1. Refer back to the Introduction to Ephesians. Who was the original audience for this letter? Write some key points about that audience on a notecard and keep it in your Bible or this book to refer back to throughout this study.

_____

_____

_____

2. Read Ephesians 1:4-5. Why might it matter to Gentile believers that God "decided in advance to adopt us into his own family?"

_____

_____

_____

3. What is God saying to you through your study of Ephesians 1:1-14?

_____

_____

_____

Go Deeper (optional):

Read Ephesians 1:8-13.

What is "the plan" that Paul speaks of?

_____

_____

According to the NLT Study Bible, "in Paul's writings, mysterious plan (traditionally mystery) often refers to a divine truth formerly hidden but now revealed in the Good News."
Thinking about the introduction we read

yesterday, why would Paul use this language of "mystery" and "knowledge" and hidden truth to speak to this audience? What would this have meant to them?

_____

_____

_____

Memory Verse:

Practice/review Ephesians 1:5. For ideas to help learn the verse, see RealWorldBible-Study.com/memory-verse-activities.

> "God decided in advance to adopt us into his own family by bringing us to himself through Jesus Christ. This is what he wanted to do, and it gave him great pleasure."
>
> — Ephesians 1:5

Prayer

Talk to God about what you think he is saying to you today. Ask for his help to live out his Word.

You may want to write your prayer here or in a journal.

* * *

Day 3: Ephesians 1:15-23

Begin with Prayer:

Invite God to speak to you as you read his Word. Ask God to help you understand, remember, and follow his Word.

Reading:

Before you begin, review your notes from day 2. Who was the original audience for this book? Now read Ephesians 1:15-23, keeping that original audience in mind.

Study:

Step 1: What did it mean "back then" when it was written?

1. Read Ephesians 1:16-20. Keep in mind that Paul is writing to believers - to established churches. Why does Paul pray for God to give them spiritual wisdom and for them to understand the "confident hope" and the "incredible greatness of God's power?" Since they are already following Christ, why would they need this wisdom and understanding?

_____

_____

_____

2. Read Ephesians 1:19-23. In "the ancient world, it was believed that there was a great cosmic struggle between the forces of good and the forces of evil. Generally, the heavens were considered to be the place where this battle between the evil rulers, principalities, powers, and ruling spirits of the universe...was being waged."[1]

When Paul tells us that Christ is now "far above any ruler or authority or power or leader or anything else," what rulers and authorities was he referring to? How would the original audience have understood this claim?

_____

----

3. What is God saying to you through your study of Ephesians 1:15-23?

Go Deeper (optional):

Thinking about all of Ephesians chapter 1, what do you think this chapter would have meant to the original hearers? List key points that would have been most significant for that audience. What did it mean for them?

Memory Verse:

Practice/review Ephesians 1:5. For ideas to help learn the verse, see RealWorldBible-Study.com/memory-verse-activities.

"God decided in advance to adopt us into his own family by bringing us to himself through Jesus Christ. This is what he wanted to do, and it gave him great pleasure."

— Ephesians 1:5

Prayer

Talk to God about what you think he is saying to you today. Ask for his help to live out his Word. You may want to write your prayer here or in a journal.

* * *

Day 4: Ephesians 1:1-23

Begin with Prayer:

Invite God to speak to you as you read his Word. Ask God to help you understand, remember, and follow his Word.

Reading:

Read Ephesians 1:1-23.

Study:

Step 2: What does it mean in the light of the rest of Scripture?

1. Read Ephesians 1:4 and 1:7, and now read Colossians 1:22, Titus 3:5-7, and Jude 1:24. How are believers made "holy and without fault in [God's] eyes?"

_____

_____

_____

2. Read Ephesians 1:19-23. Now read some or all of these verses: Ephesians 3:10, 6:12, John 12:31, Romans 8:38-39, Colossians 1:13, 2:10, and 2:15, 1 Peter 3:22, and Revelation 12:7-9. What do these verses say about the relationship (and the struggle) between Jesus and other spiritual powers?

_____

_____

_____

3. What is God saying to you through your study of Ephesians 1:1-23?

_____

_____

_____

Go Deeper (optional):

Read Ephesians 1:13-14. Now read the story of Cornelius and his family in Acts 10:1-48. What event identified Cornelius and his family as belonging to Christ? What was the impact of this event?

_____

_____

_____

Memory Verse:

Practice/review Ephesians 1:5. For ideas to help learn the verse, see RealWorldBible-Study.com/memory-verse-activities.

"God decided in advance to adopt us into his own family by bringing us to himself through Jesus Christ. This is what he wanted to do, and it gave him great pleasure."

— Ephesians 1:5

Prayer

Talk to God about what you think he is saying to you today. Ask for his help to live out his Word. You may want to write your prayer here or in a journal.

* * *

Day 5: Ephesians 1:1-23

Begin with Prayer:

Invite God to speak to you as you read his Word. Ask God to help you understand, remember, and follow his Word.

Reading:

Read Ephesians 1:1-23.

Study:

Step 3: What does it mean in my life and community?

1. Read Ephesians 1:4-5. When you think about adoption, what comes to mind? What does it mean to you personally that God "decided in advance to adopt us into his own family?"

_____

_____

_____

2. Read Ephesians 1:16-20. In what areas do you need God to grow your wisdom and understanding?

_____

_____

_____

3. What is God saying to you through your study of Ephesians 1:1-23?

_____

Go Deeper (optional):

1. Read Ephesians 1:4-7. Have you been made "holy and without fault in [God's] eyes?" Is this how you feel about your relationship with God? If you have felt differently (most of us have!), why? What would your life look like if you lived knowing this is true?

----

2. Read Ephesians 1:19-23. What does it mean for you personally that Christ is now "far above any ruler or authority or power or leader or anything else?"

----

3. Who do you know that needs to hear the truth from this chapter? What do they most need to

hear, and why? How could you tell them or remind them of this truth?

Memory Verse:

Practice/review Ephesians 1:5. For ideas to help learn the verse, see RealWorldBible-Study.com/memory-verse-activities.

> "God decided in advance to adopt us into his own family by bringing us to himself through Jesus Christ. This is what he wanted to do, and it gave him great pleasure."
>
> — Ephesians 1:5

Prayer

Talk to God about what you think he is saying to you today. Ask for his help to live out his Word. You may want to write your prayer here or in a journal.

* * *

Group Session

If you have new members or visitors, take a minute to explain the structure of this group study and what to expect each week, just like we did in the first session. You may want to bring some blank notecards for question #2 below.

Opening Prayer:

Ask God to guide your conversation as you study his Word together.

Memory Verse Activity:

Practice this verse as a group. If you need ideas for ways to practice, see the list of Memory Verse Activities at RealWorldBibleStudy.com/memory-verse-activities.

> "God decided in advance to adopt us into his own family by bringing us to himself through Jesus Christ. This is what he wanted to do, and it gave him great pleasure."

— Ephesians 1:5

Reading:

Read Ephesians 1:1-23 together as a group.

Discussion:

Use the questions below to direct your group discussion, or add your own. Make sure each group member has an opportunity to share. If you're studying independently, use the questions below for journaling/reflection.

1. What was one thing that stood out to you or surprised you as you read Ephesians 1:1-23?
2. Think about the original audience of Ephesians. Use the note card you created earlier this week to remind yourself what we know about them. (Some members of your group may not have created a notecard; this is a good time to review key points about the original audience as a group and allow members to make a reference notecard

if they have not already done so.) What would this passage have meant to the first readers and hearers?

3. What does this passage mean in the light of the rest of Scripture? Can you think of any connections to other Bible passages you have studied? Are the ideas in this passage discussed the same way across the Bible? Or are these ideas where God gives different instructions to people in different contexts?

4. Read Ephesians 1:4 and 1:7, and now read Colossians 1:22, Titus 3:5-7, and Jude 1:24. What does it mean that believers are made "holy and without fault in [God's] eyes?"

5. Are there any questions that came up during your study today or this week?

6. What does this passage mean in our lives and our community now?

7. What do you want to do this week in response to God's Word?

Prayer:

Depending on the size of your group, you may choose to pray together as a group or break off into pairs or smaller groups to share prayer requests. If you're studying independently, use this time to talk to God about what he has spoken to you through this chapter.

---

1. Patzia, 2011

Week 3: Ephesians 2

Day 1: Ephesians 2:1-10

Begin with Prayer:

Invite God to speak to you as you read his Word. Ask God to help you understand, remember, and follow his Word.

Reading:

Read Ephesians 2:1-10.

Study:

Step 1: What did it mean "back then" when it was written?

1. Reflect back on your notecard about the original audience or refer to the Introduction to Ephesians at the beginning of this book. For hearers influenced by proto-Gnostic ideas, what was the path to salvation, and who did the work to bring about salvation?

----

2. Read Ephesians 2:8-10. According to Paul, how are we saved? How is this different from the ideas in the surrounding culture?

----

3. What is God saying to you through your study of Ephesians 2:1-10?

Go Deeper (optional):

1. Read Ephesians 2:1-3. What do you think Paul means when he says "once you were dead because of your disobedience and your many sins?" According to Paul, what is the role of the devil in our lives and our choices?

_____

_____

_____

2. Read Ephesians 2:8-10. Ephesians 2:10 is quoted often. How do you understand this verse when you read what comes before it?

_____

_____

_____

Memory Verse:

Practice/review Ephesians 2:4-5. For ideas to help learn the verse, see RealWorldBible-Study.com/memory-verse-activities.

But God is so rich in mercy, and he loved us so much, that even though we were dead because of our sins, he gave us life when he raised Christ from the dead. (It is only by God's grace that you have been saved!).

— Ephesians 2:4-5

Prayer

Talk to God about what you think he is saying to you today. Ask for his help to live out his Word. You may want to write your prayer here or in a journal.

* * *

Day 2: Ephesians 2:11-22

Begin with Prayer:

Invite God to speak to you as you read his Word. Ask God to help you understand, remember, and follow his Word.

Reading:

Read Ephesians 2:11-22.

Study:

Step 1: What did it mean "back then" when it was written?

1. Read Ephesians 2:11. What do you think Paul means when he says the Jews "were proud of their circumcision, even though it affected only their bodies and not their hearts?"

_____

_____

_____

2. Reflect back on your notecard about the original audience or refer to the Introduction to Ephesians. Read Ephesians 2:14-16. What would this passage mean to the original Gentile audience as they struggled with conflict over the role of the Jewish traditions?

_____

_____

_____

3. What is God saying to you through your study of Ephesians 2:11-22?

Go Deeper (optional):

J.A. Robinson observes:

> "The Jew had a hope: The Gentile had none. The Golden age of the Gentile was in the past: his powers told him of it, and how it was gone. The Jew's golden age was in the future; his prophets told him to look forward to its coming."[1]

Read Ephesians 2:12. The Gentiles lived in a land of many "gods." How were they without God and without hope?

Memory Verse:

Practice/review Ephesians 2:4-5. For ideas to help learn the verse, see RealWorldBible-Study.com/memory-verse-activities.

> But God is so rich in mercy, and he loved us so much, that even though we were dead because of our sins, he gave us life when he raised Christ from the dead. (It is only by God's grace that you have been saved!).
>
> — Ephesians 2:4-5

Prayer

Talk to God about what you think he is saying to you today. Ask for his help to live out his Word. You may want to write your prayer here or in a journal.

* * *

Day 3: Ephesians 2:1-10

Begin with Prayer:

Invite God to speak to you as you read his Word. Ask God to help you understand, remember, and follow his Word.

Reading:

Read Ephesians 2:1-10.

Study:

Step 2: What does it mean in the light of the rest of Scripture?

1. Read Ephesians 2:1-3, and then read 2 Corinthians 4:4 and Ephesians 6:11-12. How does the devil work in the hearts of those who do not obey God? What does Paul tell believers to do in response?

----

2. Read Ephesians 2:8-9, and then read Romans 3:21-4:8, Galatians 3:2-10, 5:1-6, 2 Timothy 1:9, and Titus 3:5. Summarize the ideas from these verses. Why do you think Paul repeats these ideas so often in his letters?

_____

_____

_____

3. What is God saying to you through your study of Ephesians 2:1-10?

_____

_____

_____

Go Deeper (optional):

Read Ephesians 2:3. Then read Ephesians 5:6, Romans 1:18, 2:5, 2:8, 3:5, 5:9, 9:22, 1 Thessalonians 1:10, 5:9. What do these verses say about God's anger and judgment?

_____

_____

_____

Memory Verse:

Practice/review Ephesians 2:4-5. For ideas to help learn the verse, see RealWorldBible-Study.com/memory-verse-activities.

> But God is so rich in mercy, and he loved us so much, that even though we were dead because of our sins, he gave us life when he raised Christ from the dead. (It is only by God's grace that you have been saved!).
>
> — Ephesians 2:4-5

Prayer

Talk to God about what you think he is saying to you today. Ask for his help to live out his Word. You may want to write your prayer here or in a journal.

* * *

Day 4: Ephesians 2:11-22

Begin with Prayer:

Invite God to speak to you as you read his Word. Ask God to help you understand, remember, and follow his Word.

Reading:

Read Ephesians 2:11-22.

Study:

Step 2: What does it mean in the light of the rest of Scripture?

1. Read Ephesians 2:14-15, and then read Ephesians 1:7, Romans 3:24-25, 5:9, Colossians 1:20, Hebrews 9:12-15, 1 Peter 1:19, 1 John 1:7, Revelation 1:5 and 5:9. Summarize the main ideas from these verses. These verses were written by four different New Testament writers. What language is similar or different between them?

_____

----

2. What is God saying to you through your study of Ephesians 2:11-22?

Go Deeper (optional):

Read Ephesians 2:12. The covenants "served both a present and future function in that they established Israel ad God's special people and assured them of God's continued presence."[2]

Now read about the covenants God made with his people in Genesis 15:8-21, 17:1-21, Exodus 24:1-11, Isaiah 55:3, Jeremiah 31:31-34, and Ezekiel 37:36.

What were the covenant promises? Who were they made to?

_____

_____

Memory Verse:

Practice/review Ephesians 2:4-5. For ideas to help learn the verse, see RealWorldBible-Study.com/memory-verse-activities.

> But God is so rich in mercy, and he loved us so much, that even though we were dead because of our sins, he gave us life when he raised Christ from the dead. (It is only by God's grace that you have been saved!).
>
> — Ephesians 2:4-5

Prayer

Talk to God about what you think he is saying to you today. Ask for his help to live out his Word. You may want to write your prayer here or in a journal.

* * *

Day 5: Ephesians 2:1-22

Begin with Prayer:

Invite God to speak to you as you read his Word. Ask God to help you understand, remember, and follow his Word. .

Reading:

Read Ephesians 2:1-22.

Study:

Step 3: What does it mean in my life and community?

1. Read Ephesians 2:1-3. What does "following the passionate desires and inclinations of our sinful nature" look like in our culture? Do you remember the way you lived when "you used to live in sin, obeying the devil?" What was that life like? Is your life different now? If so, how?

----

2. Read Ephesians 2:19-20. Have you ever felt like a stranger and foreigner among God's people? How do you connect to these verses? How can we help people in our churches feel like they are "no longer strangers and foreigners" but instead "members of God's family?"

_____

_____

_____

3. What is God saying to you through your study of Ephesians 2:1-22?

_____

_____

_____

Go Deeper (optional):

1. Read Ephesians 2:8-10. Keeping in mind what we have studied about these verses this week, how are we saved? How is this similar or different to how our culture views salvation?

_____

_____

_____

2. Read Ephesians 2:11, and your responses from Day 2 about this same verse. Reflect on a time you have been proud about an outside behavior or appearance, though it didn't affect your heart.

Memory Verse:

Practice/review Ephesians 2:4-5. For ideas to help learn the verse, see RealWorldBible-Study.com/memory-verse-activities.

> But God is so rich in mercy, and he loved us so much, that even though we were dead because of our sins, he gave us life when he raised Christ from the dead. (It is only by God's grace that you have been saved!).
>
> — Ephesians 2:4-5

Prayer

Talk to God about what you think he is saying to you today. Ask for his help to live out his Word.

You may want to write your prayer here or in a journal.

* * *

Group Session

If you have new members or visitors, take a minute to explain the structure of this group study and what to expect each week, just like we did in the first session.

Opening Prayer:

Ask God to guide your conversation as you study his Word together.

Memory Verse:

Practice Ephesians 2:4-5 as a group. For ideas to help learn the verse, see RealWorldBible-Study.com/memory-verse-activities.

> But God is so rich in mercy, and he loved us so much, that even though we were dead because of our sins, he gave us life when he raised Christ from the dead. (It is

only by God's grace that you have been saved!).

— Ephesians 2:4-5

Reading:

Read Ephesians 2:1-22 together as a group.

Discussion:

Use the questions below to direct your group discussion, or add your own. Make sure each group member has an opportunity to share. If you're studying independently, use the questions below for journaling/reflection.

1. What was one thing that stood out to you or surprised you as you read Ephesians 2:1-22?
2. Think about the original audience of Ephesians. (Use your notecard as a reference, and if needed, you can turn back to the Introduction to Ephesians to remind yourself what we know about them.) What would this passage have meant to the first readers and hearers?

3. Read Ephesians 2:14-15, and then read Ephesians 1:7, Romans 3:24-25, 5:9, Colossians 1:20, Hebrews 9:12-15, 1 Peter 1:19, 1 John 1:7, Revelation 1:5 and 5:9, and review your notes from day 3 about these passages. Why do you think the New Testament writers spent so much time on this idea?
4. Are there any questions that came up during your study today or this week?
5. What does this passage mean in our lives and our community now?
6. What do you want to do this week in response to God's Word?

Prayer:

Depending on the size of your group, you may choose to pray together as a group or break off into pairs or smaller groups to share prayer requests. If you're studying independently, use this time to talk to God about what he has spoken to you through this chapter.

_____

1. Robinson, 1939
2. Patzia, 2011

Week 4: Ephesians 3:1-4:16

Day 1: Ephesians 3:1-21

Begin with Prayer:

Invite God to speak to you as you read his Word. Ask God to help you understand, remember, and follow his Word.

Reading:

Read Ephesians 3:1-21.

Study:

Step 1: What did it mean "back then" when it was written?

1. Read Ephesians 3:5-13. What is God's plan (the mystery) that has been revealed, and why would this message be important to the first readers of Ephesians? (Use your note card to remind yourself what we know about the original audience.)

_____
_____
_____

2. Who is the mystery or plan revealed to? And who is it for?

_____
_____
_____

3. What is God saying to you through your study of Ephesians 3:1-21?

_____
_____
_____

Go Deeper (optional):

1. Read Ephesians 1:21 and 3:10. What is the "all this" referred to in 3:10? What is accomplished through them?

_____

_____

_____

2. In Paul's time, "astronomers believed that...the earth was surrounded by a series of spheres that contained celestial bodies, such as the sun, moon, stars, and planets, which revolved around the earth."[1] Some religions, including Gnostics, believed that evil spirits (the "rulers and authorities" of these spheres) "needed to be placated or appeased in some way so that safe passage [for the soul] through the spheres could be guaranteed."[2] While we know the spheres aren't real, the spiritual forces and rulers are. According to Paul, what is the status of these spiritual rulers? What makes God's wisdom known to them?

_____

_____

_____

Memory Verse:

Practice/review Ephesians 3:6. For ideas to help learn the verse, see RealWorldBible-Study.com/memory-verse-activities.

> And this is God's plan: Both Gentiles and Jews who believe the Good News share equally in the riches inherited by God's children. Both are part of the same body, and both enjoy the promise of blessings because they belong to Christ Jesus.
>
> — Ephesians 3:6

Prayer

Talk to God about what you think he is saying to you today. Ask for his help to live out his Word. You may want to write your prayer here or in a journal.

* * *

Day 2: Ephesians 4:1-16

Begin with Prayer:

Invite God to speak to you as you read his Word. Ask God to help you understand, remember, and follow his Word.

Reading:

Read Ephesians 4:1-16.

Study:

Step 1: What did it mean "back then" when it was written?

1. Read Ephesians 4:1. When we read the word "therefore" (or other similar words), that is our cue to refer back to what happened in the text right before. It's a cause-and-effect word. Read Ephesians 3:14-19 (what comes before Ephesians 4:1). Based on the preceding text, why does Paul "beg you to lead a life worthy of your calling, for you have been called by God"?

_____

----

2. Read Ephesians 4:14. How do we keep from being "immature like children," and "tossed and blown about by every wind of new teaching?"

----

3. What is God saying to you through your study of Ephesians 4:1-16?

Go Deeper (optional):

1. Read Ephesians 4:1-5. How many times do you see the word "one?" The original audience of this passage worshiped the one true God, but they lived in a polytheistic culture, surrounded by people who believed in and worshiped many gods. There were gods "assigned" to every item under the sun - and even the sun itself. Need rain? Pray to the rain god. Struggling to have a

child or wanting your crops to succeed? Go to the fertility goddess. They also felt the pull to appease various spirits, as we have discussed previously. Why do you think Paul repeated the word "one" so many times in this passage?

_____

_____

_____

2. Read Ephesians 4:11-13. What are the gifts Christ gave the church? What is their responsibility, and what is the intended outcome?

_____

_____

_____

Memory Verse:

Practice/review Ephesians 3:6. For ideas to help learn the verse, see RealWorldBible-Study.com/memory-verse-activities.

And this is God's plan: Both Gentiles and Jews who believe the Good News share equally in the riches inherited by God's children. Both are part of the same body, and both enjoy the promise of blessings because they belong to Christ Jesus.

— Ephesians 3:6

Prayer

Talk to God about what you think he is saying to you today. Ask for his help to live out his Word. You may want to write your prayer here or in a journal.

* * *

Day 3: Ephesians 3:1-21

Begin with Prayer:

Invite God to speak to you as you read his Word. Ask God to help you understand, remember, and follow his Word.

Reading:

Read Ephesians 3:1-21.

Study:

Step 2: What does it mean in the light of the rest of Scripture?

1. Read Ephesians 2:14-3:13. Then read Ephesians 5:21-24, Galatians 6:16, 1 Peter 2:5,9-10, 1 Timothy 3:15, 1 Corinthians 3:16-17, 2 Corinthians 6:16, Ephesians 1:23, 4:15, 1 Corinthians 12:12-27, Colossians 1:18, 24, Ephesians 5:25-29. List the different images that the New Testament uses to describe the church and provide a brief description of each.

----

2. What is God saying to you through your study of Ephesians 3:1-21?

Go Deeper (optional):

1. Read Ephesians 3:1-13 and Colossians 1:23-2:2. List the similarities and differences between these two passages. What do you think was Paul's reason for teaching this in different ways to the Colossian church versus the more general audience of Ephesians?

_____

_____

_____

2. Read Ephesians 3:12. Then read Ephesians 2:18, Hebrews 4:14-16, 10:19-23, 1 Peter 3:18, and 1 John 4:14. Why are we now able to "come boldly and confidently into God's presence?

_____

_____

_____

Memory Verse:

Practice/review Ephesians 3:6. For ideas to help learn the verse, see RealWorldBible-Study.com/memory-verse-activities.

And this is God's plan: Both Gentiles and Jews who believe the Good News share equally in the riches inherited by God's children. Both are part of the same body, and both enjoy the promise of blessings because they belong to Christ Jesus.

— Ephesians 3:6

Prayer

Talk to God about what you think he is saying to you today. Ask for his help to live out his Word. You may want to write your prayer here or in a journal.

* * *

Day 4: Ephesians 4:1-16

Begin with Prayer:

Invite God to speak to you as you read his Word. Ask God to help you understand, remember, and follow his Word.

Reading:

Read Ephesians 4:1-16.

Study:

Step 2: What does it mean in the light of the rest of Scripture?

1. Paul has four different lists of spiritual gifts in his letters: Ephesians 4:11-12, Romans 12:4-8, 1 Corinthians 12:8, and 1 Corinthians 12:28. Read each of these lists. What are the similarities and differences? Why do you think Paul chose these specific gifts (what we call the "fivefold ministry") to emphasize in this letter?

----

2. What is the purpose of the spiritual gifts according to these passages? What is the outcome?

----

3. What is God saying to you through your study of Ephesians 4:1-16?

Go Deeper (optional):

Read Ephesians 4:11-16. Then read Galatians 1:6-7, 3:1, Colossians 2:8-23, 1 Timothy 1:3-7, 4:1-13, 6:3-5,20, 2 Timothy 4:3-4, and Titus 1:11. Why is it important to make sure we don't fall for false teaching? Why does Paul put so much emphasis on this warning, especially in his letters to Timothy and Titus (young pastors he is mentoring)? How can we identify false teaching and guard against it according to these passages?

Memory Verse:

Practice/review Ephesians 3:6. For ideas to help learn the verse, see RealWorldBible-Study.com/memory-verse-activities.

> And this is God's plan: Both Gentiles and Jews who believe the Good News share equally in the riches inherited by God's children. Both are part of the same body, and both enjoy the promise of blessings because they belong to Christ Jesus.
>
> — Ephesians 3:6

Prayer

Talk to God about what you think he is saying to you today. Ask for his help to live out his Word. You may want to write your prayer here or in a journal.

* * *

Day 5: Ephesians 3:1-4:16

Begin with Prayer:

Invite God to speak to you as you read his Word. Ask God to help you understand, remember, and follow his Word.

Reading:

Read 3:1-4:16.

Study:

Step 3: What does it mean in my life and community?

1. Read Ephesians 3:12. Do you come boldly and confidently into God's presence? What does that look like to you? If you do not, why not? What would happen if you approached God's presence that way?

----

2. Read Ephesians 4:11-16. Have you had any experience with false teachers? Where are they present in our culture? How do we guard against false teachings in our families and churches?

_____

_____

_____

3. What is God saying to you through your study of Ephesians 3:1-4:16?

_____

_____

_____

Go Deeper (optional):

Read Ephesians 4:11-12. Here are some brief definitions of these areas of leadership gifts:

- **Apostles** "were sent out as messengers, probably upon the commission of a church...to exercise leadership in spiritual and organizational matters."
- **Prophets** "received a specific message from God, either directly or through his Word, and by way of divine utterances

made the will of God known in specific situations."

- **Evangelists** were "preacher [s] of the gospel... [they] may also have the gift of making the gospel understandable or of leading individuals to accept it as God's word for them."
- **Pastors** care for the spiritual needs of the church (the "flock") as a shepherd does.
- **Teachers** are responsible for the "*feeding* of the flock through instruction."[3]

Do you identify with any of these gifts? Which ones? (If you have trouble answering this, ask the people who know you well!) Are you actively developing your gifts and using them to serve? How can you grow more in your areas of gifting?

Memory Verse:

Practice/review Ephesians 3:6. For ideas to help learn the verse, see RealWorldBible-Study.com/memory-verse-activities.

> And this is God's plan: Both Gentiles and Jews who believe the Good News share equally in the riches inherited by God's children. Both are part of the same body, and both enjoy the promise of blessings because they belong to Christ Jesus.
>
> — Ephesians 3:6

Prayer

Talk to God about what you think he is saying to you today. Ask for his help to live out his Word. You may want to write your prayer here or in a journal.

* * *

Group Session

If you have new members or visitors, take a minute to explain the structure of this group study and what to expect each week, just like we did in the first session.

Opening Prayer:

Ask God to guide your conversation as you study his Word together.

Memory Verse:

Practice Ephesians 3:6 as a group. For ideas to help learn the verse, see RealWorldBible-Study.com/memory-verse-activities.

> And this is God's plan: Both Gentiles and Jews who believe the Good News share equally in the riches inherited by God's children. Both are part of the same body, and both enjoy the promise of blessings because they belong to Christ Jesus.
>
> — Ephesians 3:6

Reading:

Read Ephesians 3:1-4:16 together as a group.

Discussion:

Use the questions below to direct your group discussion, or add your own. Make sure each group member has an opportunity to share. If you're studying independently, use the questions below for journaling/reflection.

1. What was one thing that stood out to you or surprised you as you read Ephesians 3:1-4:16?
2. Think about the original audience of Ephesians. 1. (Use your notecard as a reference, and if needed, you can turn back to the Introduction to Ephesians to remind yourself what we know about them.) What would this passage have meant to the first readers and hearers?
3. Read Ephesians 4:11-12. See below for brief definitions of these leadership gifts. Which of these gifts do each of us as a group identify with the most? What gifts do we see in each other?

4. Read Ephesians 4:11-16. What has been your group's experience with false teaching? How do we guard against it?
5. Are there any questions that came up during your study today or this week?
6. What does this passage mean in our lives and our community now?
7. What do you want to do this week in response to God's Word?

Leadership Gift Definitions:

- **Apostles** "were sent out as messengers, probably upon the commission of a church...to exercise leadership in spiritual and organizational matters."
- **Prophets** "received a specific message from God, either directly or through his Word, and by way of divine utterances made the will of God known in specific situations."
- **Evangelists** were "preacher [s] of the gospel... [they] may also have the gift of making the gospel understandable or of leading individuals to accept it as God's word for them."

- **Pastors** care for the spiritual needs of the church (the "flock") as a shepherd does.
- **Teachers** are responsible for the "*feeding* of the flock through instruction."[4]

Prayer:

Depending on the size of your group, you may choose to pray together as a group or break off into pairs or smaller groups to share prayer requests. If you're studying independently, use this time to talk to God about what he has spoken to you through this chapter.

_____

1. Patzia, 2011
2. Patzia, 2011
3. Patzia, 2011
4. Patzia, 2011

Week 5: Ephesians 4:17-5:20

Day 1: Ephesians 4:17-32

Begin with Prayer:

Invite God to speak to you as you read his Word. Ask God to help you understand, remember, and follow his Word.

Reading:

Read Ephesians 4:17-32.

Study:

Step 1: What did it mean "back then" when it was written?

1. Read Ephesians 4:17-19. According to these verses, how did the Gentiles live?

_____

_____

_____

2. Read Ephesians 4:25-32. In response to what we have learned about Christ, what behaviors should not be a part of our new life in Christ?

_____

_____

_____

3. According to Ephesians 4:25-32, what behaviors should be a part of our new life in Christ?

_____

_____

_____

4. What is God saying to you through your study of Ephesians 4:17-32?

Go Deeper (optional):

Think about the original audience (use your notecard or refer to the Introduction to Ephesians if needed). What would this passage have meant to them?

Memory Verse:

Practice/review Ephesians 4:31-32. For ideas to help learn the verse, see RealWorldBible-Study.com/memory-verse-activities.

> Get rid of all bitterness, rage, anger, harsh words, and slander, as well as all types of evil behavior. Instead, be kind to each other, tenderhearted, forgiving one another, just as God through Christ has forgiven you.

— Ephesians 4:31-32

Prayer

Talk to God about what you think he is saying to you today. Ask for his help to live out his Word. You may want to write your prayer here or in a journal.

* * *

Day 2: Ephesians 5:1-20

Begin with Prayer:

Invite God to speak to you as you read his Word. Ask God to help you understand, remember, and follow his Word.

Reading:

Read Ephesians 5:1-20.

Study:

Step 1: What did it mean "back then" when it was written?

1. Read Ephesians 5:3-7. What sins did people try to "excuse?"

_____

_____

_____

2. Reflect back on your notecard about the original audience or refer to the Introduction to Ephesians. Based on what we know about the original audience, what grounds do you think they used to try to excuse certain sins?

_____

_____

_____

3. What is God saying to you through your study of Ephesians 5:1-20?

_____

_____

_____

Go Deeper (optional):

Read Ephesians 5:1-20. Make two lists: things we *should* do and things we should *not* do according to this passage. Which of these items was a surprise to you? Which is the most difficult for you?

_____

_____

_____

Memory Verse:

Practice/review Ephesians 4:31-32. For ideas to help learn the verse, see RealWorldBible-Study.com/memory-verse-activities.

> Get rid of all bitterness, rage, anger, harsh words, and slander, as well as all types of evil behavior. Instead, be kind to each other, tenderhearted, forgiving one another, just as God through Christ has forgiven you.
>
> — Ephesians 4:31-32

Prayer

Talk to God about what you think he is saying to you today. Ask for his help to live out his Word. You may want to write your prayer here or in a journal.

* * *

Day 3: Ephesians 4:17-32

Begin with Prayer:

Invite God to speak to you as you read his Word. Ask God to help you understand, remember, and follow his Word.

Reading:

Read Ephesians 4:17-32.

Study:

Step 2: What does it mean in the light of the rest of Scripture?

1. Read Ephesians 4:21-24. Now read Romans 6:12-14, 12:2. What do these verses tell us? How do we keep from being pulled into sin by the sinful nature?

_____

_____

_____

2. Read Ephesians 4:29. Now read Ephesians 5:3-4 and James 3:3-12. Summarize what these verses say about the words we use. Which part of this is easiest for you? What part is the most challenging?

_____

_____

_____

3. What is God saying to you through your study of Ephesians 4:17-32?

_____

_____

_____

Go Deeper (optional):

Read Ephesians 4:17-18. Now read Matthew 13:15, John 12:40, 2 Corinthians 4:4, 2

Corinthians 3:13-15, Exodus 8:15, 8:32, 14:4, Hebrews 3:13. Summarize these verses. What do you think is the relationship between individuals hardening their hearts and God hardening someone's heart? (For further reading, see "A Hardened Heart" in the NLT Study Bible).

Memory Verse:

Practice/review Ephesians 4:31-32. For ideas to help learn the verse, see RealWorldBible-Study.com/memory-verse-activities.

Get rid of all bitterness, rage, anger, harsh words, and slander, as well as all types of evil behavior. Instead, be kind to each other, tenderhearted, forgiving one another, just as God through Christ has forgiven you.

— Ephesians 4:31-32

Prayer

Talk to God about what you think he is saying to you today. Ask for his help to live out his Word. You may want to write your prayer here or in a journal.

* * *

Day 4: Ephesians 5:1-20

Begin with Prayer:

Invite God to speak to you as you read his Word. Ask God to help you understand, remember, and follow his Word.

Reading:

Read Ephesians 5:1-20.

Study:

Step 2: What does it mean in the light of the rest of Scripture?

1. Read Ephesians 5:15-20. Now read Galatians 5:16-26. How is it possible for us to live the way Ephesians tells us to live (and to avoid the sinful behaviors Ephesians tells us to avoid)?

_____

_____

_____

2. Read Ephesians 5:1-2. Now read John 15:13 and Romans 5:8. How are we to imitate God?

_____

_____

_____

3. What is God saying to you through your study of Ephesians 5:1-20?

_____

_____

_____

Go Deeper (optional):

Read Ephesians 5:10-15. Now read Isaiah 52:1-3. "Awake, o sleeper" might "be a fragment from an unknown Christian song, perhaps based on texts in Isaiah"[1] such as the one above. What do you think Paul meant by quoting this song here?

_____

_____

_____

Memory Verse:

Practice/review Ephesians 4:31-32. For ideas to help learn the verse, see RealWorldBible-Study.com/memory-verse-activities.

> Get rid of all bitterness, rage, anger, harsh words, and slander, as well as all types of evil behavior. Instead, be kind to each other, tenderhearted, forgiving one another, just as God through Christ has forgiven you.
>
> — Ephesians 4:31-32

Prayer

Talk to God about what you think he is saying to you today. Ask for his help to live out his Word. You may want to write your prayer here or in a journal.

* * *

Day 5: Ephesians 4:17-5:20

Begin with Prayer:

Invite God to speak to you as you read his Word. Ask God to help you understand, remember, and follow his Word.

Reading:

Read Ephesians 4:17-5:20.

Study:

Step 3: What does it mean in my life and community?

1. Read Ephesians 4:17-19. Who in our culture would be the equivalent of the Gentiles? How do they live?

_____

_____

_____

2. Read Ephesians 5:6-9. What are some sins that our culture tries to "excuse?" What should our response be?

_____

_____

_____

3. What does Ephesians 4:17-5:20 mean for your life and community? What is God saying to you through your study of Ephesians 4:17-5:20?

_____

_____

_____

Go Deeper (optional):

Read Ephesians 4:19 in the alternate translations below:

Having lost all sensitivity, they have given themselves over to sensuality so as to indulge in every kind of impurity, and they are full of greed.

— Ephesians 4:19 (NIV)

They are people who lack all sense of right and wrong, and who have turned themselves over to doing whatever feels good and to practicing every sort of corruption along with greed.

— Ephesians 4:19 (CEB)

Do you ever lose sensitivity to sin, or to right and wrong, in our culture? How do we keep from doing this?

Memory Verse:

Practice/review Ephesians 4:31-32. For ideas to help learn the verse, see RealWorldBible-Study.com/memory-verse-activities.

> Get rid of all bitterness, rage, anger, harsh words, and slander, as well as all types of evil behavior. Instead, be kind to each other, tenderhearted, forgiving one another, just as God through Christ has forgiven you.
>
> — Ephesians 4:31-32

Prayer

Talk to God about what you think he is saying to you today. Ask for his help to live out his Word. You may want to write your prayer here or in a journal.

Group Session

If you have new members or visitors, take a minute to explain the structure of this group study and what to expect each week, just like we did in the first session.

Opening Prayer:

Ask God to guide your conversation as you study his Word together.

Memory Verse:

Practice Ephesians 4:31-32 as a group. For ideas to help learn the verse, see RealWorldBible-Study.com/memory-verse-activities.

> Get rid of all bitterness, rage, anger, harsh words, and slander, as well as all types of evil behavior. Instead, be kind to each other, tenderhearted, forgiving one another, just as God through Christ has forgiven you.
>
> — Ephesians 4:31-32

Reading:

Read Ephesians 4:17-5:20 together as a group.

Discussion:

Use the questions below to direct your group discussion, or add your own. Make sure each group member has an opportunity to share. If you're studying independently, use the questions below for journaling/reflection.

1. What was one thing that stood out to you or surprised you as you read Ephesians 4:17-5:20?

2. This passage deals quite a bit with ethics - how we live. Think about the original audience of Ephesians. (If needed, you can use your notecard or turn back to the Introduction to Ephesians to remind yourself what we know about them.) What would this passage have meant to the first readers and hearers?

3. Read Ephesians 5:15-20. Now read Galatians 5:16-26. How is it possible for us to live the way Ephesians tells us to

live (and to avoid the sinful behaviors Ephesians tells us to avoid)?

4. Can you think of any other verses or passages in Scripture with similar themes to this one? What do they have in common? How are they different?
5. Are there any questions that came up during your study today or this week?
6. What does this passage mean in our lives and our community now?
7. What do you want to do this week in response to God's Word?

Prayer:

Depending on the size of your group, you may choose to pray together as a group or break off into pairs or smaller groups to share prayer requests. If you're studying independently, use this time to talk to God about what he has spoken to you through this chapter.

_____

1. Tyndale, 2008

Week 6: Ephesians 5:21-6:9

Day 1: Ephesians 5:21-33

Begin with Prayer:

Invite God to speak to you as you read his Word. Ask God to help you understand, remember, and follow his Word.

Reading:

Read Ephesians 5:21-33.

Study:

Step 1: What did it mean "back then" when it was written?

1. Read Ephesians 5:18-21. The "and further" in this verse is a cue that we need to look to the previous section to make the connection. Here, "the verb form links it with the command to be filled" (5:18). What are the different components listed here of living a life filled with the Holy Spirit?

_____

_____

_____

2. Who is called to submit according to Ephesians 5:21?

_____

_____

_____

3. What is God saying to you through your study of Ephesians 5:21-33?

_____

_____

_____

Go Deeper (optional):

Read Ephesians 5:21-33. How does this passage describe Spirit-guided relationships between husbands and wives? What are the instructions to each partner? List out the individual instructions in each verse:

- 5:21
- 5:22-24
- 5:25
- 5:28
- 5:31
- 5:33

Memory Verse:

Practice/review Ephesians 5:21. For ideas to help learn the verse, see RealWorldBible-Study.com/memory-verse-activities.

> And further, submit to one another out of reverence for Christ.
>
> — Ephesians 5:21

Prayer

Talk to God about what you think he is saying to you today. Ask for his help to live out his Word. You may want to write your prayer here or in a journal.

* * *

Day 2: Ephesians 6:1-9

Begin with Prayer:

Invite God to speak to you as you read his Word. Ask God to help you understand, remember, and follow his Word.

Reading:

Read Ephesians 6:1-9.

Study:

Step 1: What did it mean "back then" when it was written?

1. Read Ephesians 6:1-9. What instructions does Paul give to each household member (children, fathers/parents, slaves, masters)?

_____

_____

_____

2. How do these verses tie back with the beginning of this section, Ephesians 5:18-21?

_____

_____

_____

3. What is God saying to you through your study of Ephesians 6:1-9?

_____

_____

_____

Go Deeper (optional):

The "Greco Roman slave system was integral part of every of aspect of life in Paul's time. Estimates are that 85-90 percent of the inhabitants of Rome and peninsula Italy were slaves or of slave origin in the first and second centuries A.D...by law slaves were what Aristotle called 'human tools.'"[1]

Given the position of slavery during Paul's time, why do you think he included these instructions towards slaves and masters in Ephesians? How would the original audience have received or understood them?

_____

_____

_____

Memory Verse:

Practice/review Ephesians 5:21. For ideas to help learn the verse, see RealWorldBible-Study.com/memory-verse-activities.

> And further, submit to one another out of reverence for Christ.
>
> — Ephesians 5:21

Prayer

Talk to God about what you think he is saying to you today. Ask for his help to live out his Word. You may want to write your prayer here or in a journal.

* * *

Day 3: Ephesians 5:21-33

Begin with Prayer:

Invite God to speak to you as you read his Word. Ask God to help you understand, remember, and follow his Word.

Reading:

Read Ephesians 5:21-33.

Study:

Step 2: What does it mean in the light of the rest of Scripture?

1. Read Ephesians 5:21-33. Now read Colossians 3:18-19, Matthew 19:4-6, and 1 Peter 3:1-7. What do these passages have in common? How are they different? Summarize what these passages teach. What reasons does Paul give for the relationships between husbands and wives?

_____

_____

_____

2. What is God saying to you through your study of Ephesians 5:21-33?

_____

_____

_____

Go Deeper (optional):

Read Ephesians 5:25-30. Now read Isaiah 62:4-5, 2 Corinthians 11:1-4, Isaiah 54:5, Revelation 19:6-9, and Revelation 21:1-2. Scripture refers to the church as the Bride of Christ, and the Old Testament frequently identifies the people of Israel as a bride (see also Hosea). How do these verses describe the church? How does this imagery help us understand our relationship with Jesus?

_____

_____

_____

Memory Verse:

Practice/review Ephesians 5:21. For ideas to help learn the verse, see RealWorldBible-Study.com/memory-verse-activities.

> And further, submit to one another out of reverence for Christ.
>
> — Ephesians 5:21

Prayer

Talk to God about what you think he is saying to you today. Ask for his help to live out his Word. You may want to write your prayer here or in a journal.

* * *

Day 4: Ephesians 6:1-9

Begin with Prayer:

Invite God to speak to you as you read his Word. Ask God to help you understand, remember, and follow his Word.

Reading:

Read Ephesians 6:1-9.

Study:

Step 2: What does it mean in the light of the rest of Scripture?

1. Read Ephesians 6:1-3. Paul quotes Exodus 20:12 (from the Ten Commandments); read Exodus 20:1-17 to understand the original commandment in context. Who is the original commandment for? Who is Paul's instruction directed to in Ephesians 6:1? What are the similarities and differences between the two instructions?

----

2. What is God saying to you through your study of Ephesians 6:1-9?

Go Deeper (optional):

1. Use a concordance to search for the word "child/children" or "slave." Read as many verses as you can. (You'll need to read each verse in context - with the surrounding verses - to make sure it applies to today's reading.) Summarize what you find: what is God's attitude and heart toward children and/or slaves? What are his commandments regarding them?

----

2. Read Ephesians 6:4. Now read Deuteronomy

4:9, Deuteronomy 6:7-9, 20-25, Psalm 34:11, Proverbs 13:24, 19:18, 22:6 Colossians 3:21, Hebrews 12:5-11, 1 Timothy 3:1-5. Summarize the parents' responsibilities in these verses.

Memory Verse:

Practice/review Ephesians 5:21. For ideas to help learn the verse, see RealWorldBible-Study.com/memory-verse-activities.

> And further, submit to one another out of reverence for Christ.
>
> — Ephesians 5:21

Prayer

Talk to God about what you think he is saying to you today. Ask for his help to live out his Word. You may want to write your prayer here or in a journal.

* * *

Day 5: Ephesians 5:21-6:9

Begin with Prayer:

Invite God to speak to you as you read his Word. Ask God to help you understand, remember, and follow his Word.

Reading:

Read Ephesians 5:21-6:9.

Study:

Step 3: What does it mean in my life and community?

1. Read Ephesians 5:21-33. How do you think this passage applies in our culture? If you are married or preparing for marriage, what does this passage teach you?

_____

_____

_____

2. Read Ephesians 6:5-9. How would this instruction apply to our culture where slavery is no longer legal and we are not in "slave/master" relationships? Which relationships in our lives would be similar enough to apply this instruction?

_____

_____

_____

3. What is God saying to you through your study of Ephesians 5:21-6:9?

_____

_____

_____

Go Deeper (optional):

Which of the instructions represented in Ephesians 5:21-6:9 is the easiest for you to carry out? Which is the most difficult, and why?

_____

_____

_____

How can you grow in Spirit-guided relationships based on what you have studied this week?

_____

_____

_____

Memory Verse:

Practice/review Ephesians 5:21. For ideas to help learn the verse, see RealWorldBible-Study.com/memory-verse-activities.

> And further, submit to one another out of reverence for Christ.
>
> — Ephesians 5:21

Prayer

Talk to God about what you think he is saying to you today. Ask for his help to live out his Word. You may want to write your prayer here or in a journal.

Group Session

If you have new members or visitors, take a minute to explain the structure of this group study and what to expect each week, just like we did in the first session.

Opening Prayer:

Ask God to guide your conversation as you study his Word together.

Memory Verse:

Practice Ephesians 5:21 as a group. For ideas to help learn the verse, see RealWorldBible-Study.com/memory-verse-activities.

> And further, submit to one another out of reverence for Christ.
>
> — Ephesians 5:21

Reading:

Read Ephesians 5:21-6:9 together as a group.

Discussion:

Use the questions below to direct your group discussion, or add your own. Make sure each group member has an opportunity to share. If you're studying independently, use the questions below for journaling/reflection.

1. What was one thing that stood out to you or surprised you as you read Ephesians 5:21-6:9?

2. Think about the original audience of Ephesians. (Use your notecard or you can turn back to the Introduction to Ephesians to remind yourself what we know about them.) What would this passage have meant to the first readers and hearers? How would this teaching be similar or different from what the culture was telling those hearers? (Keep in mind that this is what we call "ethical" teaching. What issues around ethics would that first audience be working through according to the Introduction to Ephesians?)

3. Read Ephesians 6:1-3. Paul quotes Exodus 20:12 (from the Ten

Commandments); read Exodus 20:1-17 to understand the original commandment in context. What do you think is the difference between "honoring" and "obeying" parents? What do you think about the fact that this commandment is part of the Ten

4. Are there any questions that came up during your study today or this week?

5. Which of the instructions represented in Ephesians 5:21-6:9 is the easiest for you to carry out? Which is the most difficult, and why? How can you grow in Spirit-guided relationships based on what you have studied this week?

6. What do you want to do this week in response to God's Word?

Prayer:

Depending on the size of your group, you may choose to pray together as a group or break off into pairs or smaller groups to share prayer requests. If you're studying independently, use this time to talk to God about what he has spoken to you through this chapter.

Ephesians

1. Hawthorne, et al., 1993

Week 7: Ephesians 6:10-24

Day 1: Ephesians 6:10-14

Begin with Prayer:

Invite God to speak to you as you read his Word. Ask God to help you understand, remember, and follow his Word.

Reading:

Read Ephesians 6:10-14.

Study:

Step 1: What did it mean "back then" when it was written?

1. Read Ephesians 6:14. Have you ever heard the phrase "gird your loins?" It means, "get ready." Ephesians 6:14 literally says, "gird your loins with truth." When a Roman soldier put on the belt, which would hold a sword or dagger and included a bronze apron to protect the loin area, it meant he was ready for battle. With this in mind, what do you think it means to put on the belt of truth?

_____
_____
_____

2. Read Ephesians 6:14. The "body armor" or "breastplate" covered the chest and protected the heart and other internal organs–all the gooey stuff you really can't afford to lose. And "righteousness" simply refers to "right living." What role does "right living" play in spiritual warfare according to this verse?

_____
_____

----

3. What is God saying to you through your study of Ephesians 6:10-14?

Go Deeper (optional):

1. Read Ephesians 6:11, and refer to the historical context in the Introduction to Ephesians. You may also want to skim through the book of Acts which tells the story of the early church including many of their struggles. What were some of the common "strategies" or "schemes" of the devil during Paul's time?

----

2. The book of Proverbs in the Bible is a collection of wise sayings. Browse through Proverbs and list as many verses as you can find that talk about honesty, integrity, or lying.

Memory Verse:

Practice/review Ephesians 6:12-13. For ideas to help learn the verse, see RealWorldBible-Study.com/memory-verse-activities.

> For we are not fighting against flesh-and-blood enemies, but against evil rulers and authorities of the unseen world, against mighty powers in this dark world, and against evil spirits in the heavenly places. Therefore, put on every piece of God's armor so you will be able to resist the enemy in the time of evil. Then after the battle you will still be standing firm.
>
> — Ephesians 6:12-13

Prayer

Talk to God about what you think he is saying to you today. Ask for his help to live out his Word. You may want to write your prayer here or in a journal.

* * *

Day 2: Ephesians 6:15-18

Begin with Prayer:

Invite God to speak to you as you read his Word. Ask God to help you understand, remember, and follow his Word.

Reading:

Read Ephesians 6:15-18.

Study:

Step 1: What did it mean "back then" when it was written?

1. Read Ephesians 6:15. Ancient Roman soldiers wore strapped sandals with thick leather soles. They had spikes in the bottoms to provide better traction and help the soldier stand his ground in hand to hand combat. These leather shoes grew more comfortable with constant wear. How do

the "shoes" of God's peace help us in spiritual
battle?

_____

_____

_____

2. Read Ephesians 6:16. The shield was covered
with leather, and soldiers would often soak it
with water before going into battle, to extinguish
flaming arrows and prevent them from setting
the shield afire. Even though the shield is a
defensive piece of armor, soldiers used it in an
active way, moving this way or that to block
specific blows from the enemy. What is the role
of faith in spiritual warfare?

_____

_____

_____

3. What is God saying to you through your study
of Ephesians 6:15-18?

_____

_____

_____

Go Deeper (optional):

Spiritual combat is hand-to-hand combat, and there is only one offensive weapon in God's Armor. The Sword of the Spirit, God's Word, is both defensive and offensive. We can use it both to defend against the enemy's attacks and to attack the enemy ourselves. We will always play defense, because Satan wants to get in the way of God's plans every day. He doesn't know how to give up! But if we want to get out of survival mode, we need to go on the offensive. To do this, we have to learn how to use that sword!

5 Ways to Use your Sword:

- Study God's Word so you grow in faith and knowledge of God, and apply it to your life.
- Memorize Bible verses and learn Bible stories, and use them to defend against Satan's attacks.
- Pray through Bible verses to grow in your prayer walk.
- Rebuke Satan with Scripture.

- Practice "sword drills" (looking up verses) so you get really good at finding things in your Bible.

Which of these have you used before? Which would you like to try?

_____

_____

_____

Memory Verse:

Practice/review Ephesians 6:12-13. For ideas to help learn the verse, see RealWorldBible-Study.com/memory-verse-activities.

> For we are not fighting against flesh-and-blood enemies, but against evil rulers and authorities of the unseen world, against mighty powers in this dark world, and against evil spirits in the heavenly places. Therefore, put on every piece of God's armor so you will be able to resist the enemy in the time of evil. Then after the battle you will still be standing firm.

— Ephesians 6:12-13

Prayer

Talk to God about what you think he is saying to you today. Ask for his help to live out his Word. You may want to write your prayer here or in a journal.

* * *

Day 3: Ephesians 6:10-14

Begin with Prayer:

Invite God to speak to you as you read his Word. Ask God to help you understand, remember, and follow his Word.

Reading:

Read Ephesians 6:10-14.

Study:

Step 2: What does it mean in the light of the rest of Scripture?

1. Read Ephesians 6:10-18. Now read Ephesians 4:27, James 4:7, Romans 8:38-39, 1 Corinthians 15:24. What are Christians called to in response to the enemy? What confidence can we have as we follow this instruction?

_____

_____

_____

2. As we discussed on Day 1, the "body armor" or "breastplate" covered the chest and protected the heart and other internal organs – all the gooey stuff you really can't afford to lose. And "righteousness" simply refers to "right living." You guard your heart with right living. Read Proverbs 4:23 and Philippians 4:6-7. What's another way we can guard our hearts according to Philippians?

_____

_____

_____

3. What is God saying to you through your study of Ephesians 6:10-14?

_____

_____

_____

Go Deeper (optional):

Read or listen to Judges 6:1-7:22, 8:22-8:28. Why did God allow the Midianites to invade and terrorize the Israelites in this story? The Israelites didn't just instantly start worshipping other gods. They started to bend the rules slightly here and there, and took part in behaviors that invited Satan's influence in their lives. The way they lived made them vulnerable to Satan's attack. How have you experienced this in your own life?

_____

_____

_____

Memory Verse:

Practice/review Ephesians 6:12-13. For ideas to help learn the verse, see RealWorldBible-Study.com/memory-verse-activities.

> For we are not fighting against flesh-and-blood enemies, but against evil rulers and authorities of the unseen world, against mighty powers in this dark world, and against evil spirits in the heavenly places. Therefore, put on every piece of God's armor so you will be able to resist the enemy in the time of evil. Then after the battle you will still be standing firm.
>
> — Ephesians 6:12-13

Prayer

Talk to God about what you think he is saying to you today. Ask for his help to live out his Word. You may want to write your prayer here or in a journal.

* * *

Day 4: Ephesians 6:15-18

Begin with Prayer:

Invite God to speak to you as you read his Word. Ask God to help you understand, remember, and follow his Word.

Reading:

Read Ephesians 6:15-18.

Study:

Step 2: What does it mean in the light of the rest of Scripture?

1. Read Ephesians 6:15. Now read Philippians 4:6-7. How do we get God's peace? What will God's peace do in our lives?

_____

_____

_____

2. Read Ephesians 6:17. The helmet guards our heads: our minds and our thought life with our

knowledge of the gospel and our hope in Christ. When we are tempted to think or do something wrong, the knowledge of Jesus' victory on the cross on our behalf can remind us we never have to go back to those old ways. And when the enemy pesters us with guilt and shame about what we have done in the past, we have to put on the helmet of salvation. When Jesus died for me on the cross, he finished the job. The forgiveness I have in him is complete, and there is no more shame. Read 2 Timothy 1:9, Titus 2:11-12, and 1 John 1:9. How should we live in response to God's salvation? When we realized we have sinned, how should we respond? What will happen when we do?

----

3. What is God saying to you through your study of Ephesians 6:15-18?

Go Deeper (optional):

1. Read John 3:17 and 2 Corinthians 5:17. When you have sinned, and asked God's forgiveness, but still feel shame and condemnation, where do those feelings come from? How can you respond to those feelings?

_____

_____

_____

2. Read Ephesians 6:16 and read or listen to Hebrews 11, the "faith hall of fame." According to Hebrews 11:1, what is the definition of faith?

_____

_____

_____

Memory Verse:

Practice/review Ephesians 6:12-13. For ideas to help learn the verse, see RealWorldBible-Study.com/memory-verse-activities.

For we are not fighting against flesh-and-blood enemies, but against evil rulers and authorities of the unseen world, against mighty powers in this dark world, and against evil spirits in the heavenly places. Therefore, put on every piece of God's armor so you will be able to resist the enemy in the time of evil. Then after the battle you will still be standing firm.

— Ephesians 6:12-13

Prayer

Talk to God about what you think he is saying to you today. Ask for his help to live out his Word. You may want to write your prayer here or in a journal.

* * *

Day 5: Ephesians 6:10-24

Begin with Prayer:

Invite God to speak to you as you read his Word. Ask God to help you understand, remember, and follow his Word.

Reading:

Read Ephesians 6:10-24.

Study:

Step 3: What does it mean in my life and community?

1. Read Ephesians 6:10-11. What "schemes" or "strategies" has the enemy used against you recently? Choose from those listed or write your own:

- Disunity
- Personal Sin
- Unforgiveness
- False teachers
- Discouragement
- Apathy (not caring one way or the other)
- Suffering
- Fear
- Accusation
- Laziness
- Gossip
- "You're not good enough."

2. Read Ephesians 6:13-18. Which piece of God's armor do you struggle with putting on (or even remembering to put on!) each day? Which do you need most in this season?

_____

_____

_____

3. What is God saying to you through your study of Ephesians 6:10-24?

_____

_____

_____

Go Deeper (optional):

1. Read Ephesians 6:16. What are some of the "blows" that have been sent your way recently? What are some of the flaming arrows Satan likes to throw at you? (This could be a particular sin, or something that discourages you, or even a person who pushes your buttons.)

_____

_____

_____

2. How can the shield of faith help you extinguish these flaming arrows?

_____

_____

_____

Memory Verse:

Practice/review Ephesians 6:12-13. For ideas to help learn the verse, see RealWorldBible-Study.com/memory-verse-activities.

> For we are not fighting against flesh-and-blood enemies, but against evil rulers and authorities of the unseen world, against mighty powers in this dark world, and against evil spirits in the heavenly places. Therefore, put on every piece of God's armor so you will be able to resist the enemy in the time of evil. Then after the battle you will still be standing firm.
>
> — Ephesians 6:12-13

Prayer

Talk to God about what you think he is saying to you today. Ask for his help to live out his Word. You may want to write your prayer here or in a journal.

Group Session

If you have new members or visitors, take a minute to explain the structure of this group study and what to expect each week, just like we did in the first session.

Opening Prayer:

Ask God to guide your conversation as you study his Word together.

Memory Verse:

Practice Ephesians 6:12-13 as a group. For ideas to help learn the verse, see RealWorldBible-Study.com/memory-verse-activities.

For we are not fighting against flesh-and-blood enemies, but against evil rulers and authorities of the unseen world, against mighty powers in this dark world, and against evil spirits in the heavenly places. Therefore, put on every piece of God's armor so you will be able to resist the enemy in the time of evil. Then after the battle you will still be standing firm.

— Ephesians 6:12-13

Reading:

Read Ephesians 6:10-24 together as a group.

Discussion:

Use the questions below to direct your group discussion, or add your own. Make sure each group member has an opportunity to share. If you're studying independently, use the questions below for journaling/reflection.

1. Refer back to the descriptions of each piece of the Armor of God on days 1 and 2 of this week's study. What was one

thing that stood out to you or surprised you as you read Ephesians 6:10-24 or as you read through these descriptions?

2. Think about the original audience of Ephesians. (Use your bookmark for reference or turn back to the Introduction to Ephesians to remind yourself what we know about them.) What would this passage have meant to the first readers and hearers?

3. Which piece of God's armor do you struggle with putting on (or even remembering to put on!) each day? Which do you need most in your life?

4. Which part of wearing the belt of truth (living a truthful life) is harder for you, being honest (not telling lies) or being open? Do you have someone in your life you can be open and vulnerable with?

5. Where in your life do you especially need God's peace right now?

6. Are there any questions that came up during your study today or this week?

7. What does this passage mean in our lives and our community now?

8. What do you want to do this week in response to God's Word?

Prayer:

Depending on the size of your group, you may choose to pray together as a group or break off into pairs or smaller groups to share prayer requests. If you're studying independently, use this time to talk to God about what he has spoken to you through this chapter.

Bibliography

Fee, Gordon D. *How to Read the Bible Book by Book: A Guided Tour*. Zondervan, 2009.

Fee, Gordon D., and Douglas K. Stuart. *How to Read the Bible for All Its Worth*. Fourth edition. Grand Rapids, Michigan: Zondervan, 2014.

Hawthorne, Gerald F. 1925-, Ralph P. Martin, Daniel G. 1949- Reid, Gerald F. 1925- Hawthorne, Ralph P. Martin, and Daniel G. 1949- Reid. *Dictionary of Paul and His Letters*. The IVP Bible Dictionary Series; [7]. Downers Grove, Ill.: InterVarsity Press, 1993. http://www.gbv.de/dms/hebis-mainz/toc/02933229X.pdf.

Klein, William W. (William Wade), Tremper Longman, David E. Garland, Arthur A. Rupprecht, and Todd D. Still. *The Expositor's Bible Commentary. Ephesians, Philippians, Colossians, Philemon*. Revised edition. 1 online resource vols. Grand Rapids, Michigan: Zondervan, 2017. https://nls.ldls.org.uk/welcome.html?ark:/81055/vdc_100059762492.0x000001.

Köstenberger, Andreas J. 1957-, Arthur A. Rupprecht, and Wood, A.Skevington. *The Expositor's Bible Commentary: Ephesians-Philemon*. Revised edition. The Expositor's Bible Commentary, Revised Edition. Grand Rapids, Mich.: Zondervan, 2006.

Longman, Tremper III., and David E. Garland. *The Expositor's Bible Commentary*. Rev. ed. Expositor's Bible Commentary (Rev. Ed.). Grand Rapids, Mich.: Zondervan, 2006. http://catdir.loc.gov/catdir/enhancements/fy0642/2005006281-s.html.

Patzia, Arthur G. *Ephesians, Colossians, Philemon*.

Bibliography

Understanding the Bible Commentary Series. Grand Rapids: BakerBooks, 2011.

Robinson, J. Armitage (Joseph Armitage), 1858-1933. *St. Paul's Epistle to the Ephesians: An Exposition*. London: Macmillan, 1939.

Stamps, Donald. *Fire Bible: Global Study Edition*. New international version. Hendrickson Pub, 2010.

Tyndale. *NLT Study Bible*. Tyndale House Publishers, Inc., 2008.

Utley, Robert James. *Paul Bound, the Gospel Unbound: Letters from Prison (Colossians, Ephesians and Philemon, Then Later, Philippians)*. Vol. Volume 8. Study Guide Commentary Series. Marshall, TX: Bible Lessons International, 1997.

Westcott, Brooke Foss, and Fenton John Anthony Hort. *The New Testament in the Original Greek*. Logos Bible Software, 2009.

Wright, N. T. (Nicholas Thomas), and N. T. (Nicholas Thomas) Wright. *Paul for Everyone: The Prison Letters: Ephesians, Philippians, Colossians, and Philemon*. [2nd ed.]. New Testament for Everyone. London: SPCK;, 2004.

About the Author

Joy Suzanne Hunt is the Pastor of Adult Education for CityWide Mosaic Church in Temecula, CA and a professor with SoCal School of Ministry. Her mission is to equip men and women to take ownership of their lives, faith, and finances. When she's not teaching, writing, or coaching, you can find her walking her Temecula neighborhood, trying out crockpot recipes, or playing board games with friends.

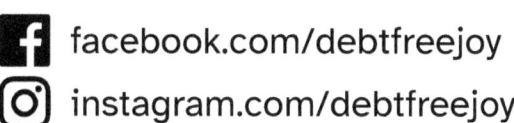

facebook.com/debtfreejoy

instagram.com/debtfreejoy